MARS

MURRAY "OAK" TAPETA

NORWOOD HOUSE  PRESS

Cataloging-in-Publication Data

Names: Tapeta, Murray.
Title: Mars / Murray Tapeta.
Description: Buffalo, NY : Norwood House Press, 2026. | Series: Outer space | Includes glossary and index.
Identifiers: ISBN 9781978574830 (pbk.) | ISBN 9781978574847 (library bound) | ISBN 9781978574854 (ebook)
Subjects: LCSH: Mars (Planet)--Juvenile literature.
Classification: LCC QB641.T374 2026 | DDC 523.43--dc23

Published in 2026 by
Norwood House Press
2544 Clinton Street
Buffalo, NY 14224

Designer: Rhea Magaro
Editor: Kim Thompson

Photo credits: Cover, pp. 1, 5, 9, 12, 13, 18, 19 NASA; p. 6 buradaki/Shutterstock.com; p. 7 Andrey Yurlov/Shutterstock.com; p. 8 itechno/Shutterstock.com; p. 11 Elena/Shutterstock.com; p. 14 Roman Samborskyi/Shutterstock.com; p. 16 Vadim Sadovski/Shutterstock.com; p. 17 Krivosheev Vitaly/Shutterstock.com; p. 21 Frame Stock Footage /Shutterstock.com;

Printed in the United States of America

CPSIA compliance information: Batch #CSNHP26: For further information contact Norwood House Press at 1-800-237-9932.

TABLE OF CONTENTS

Where Is Mars? 4
How Was Mars Discovered? 8
What Is It Like on Mars? 10
Has Mars Been Explored? 18
Glossary 22
Thinking Questions 23
Index 24
About the Author 24

Where Is Mars?

Our **solar system** has eight planets. Mars is the fourth planet from the Sun. It is about half the size of Earth.

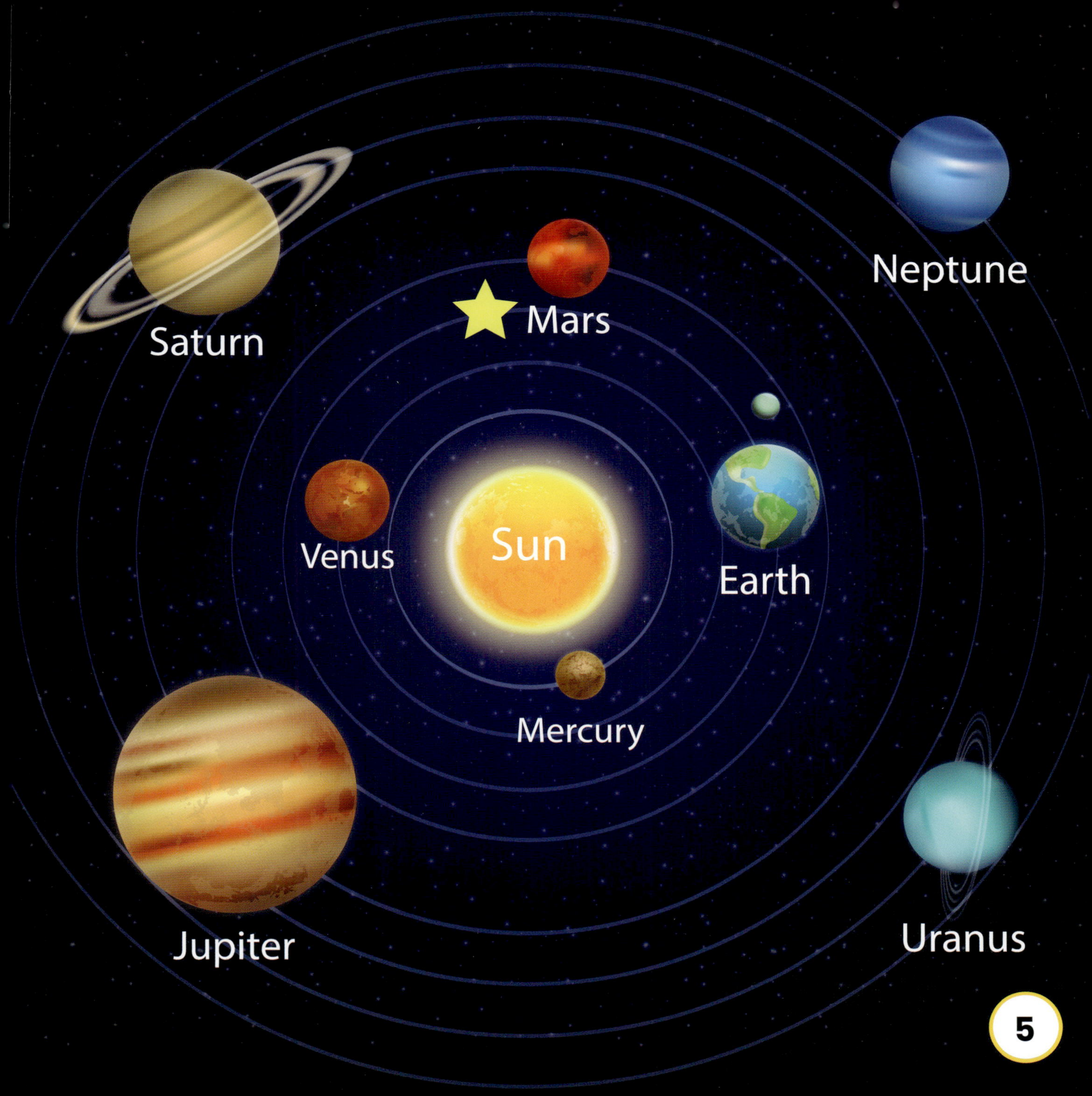
Neptune
Mars
Saturn
Venus
Sun
Earth
Mercury
Jupiter
Uranus

Mars is about 142 million miles (228 million kilometers) away from the Sun. Traveling from Earth to Mars would take over a month.

One year on Mars is 687 Earth days long.
It takes Mars that long to **orbit** the Sun.

How Was Mars Discovered?

Ancient people noticed Mars when they looked up at the stars. They saw a bright red dot. It reminded them of blood. They named the planet Mars after the Roman god of war.

Italian **astronomer** Galileo Galilei first saw Mars through a **telescope** in 1610.

What Is It Like on Mars?

Mars is a **terrestrial** planet. It is cold, dry, and rocky. The surface is covered with reddish dust. Mars is called "the red planet."

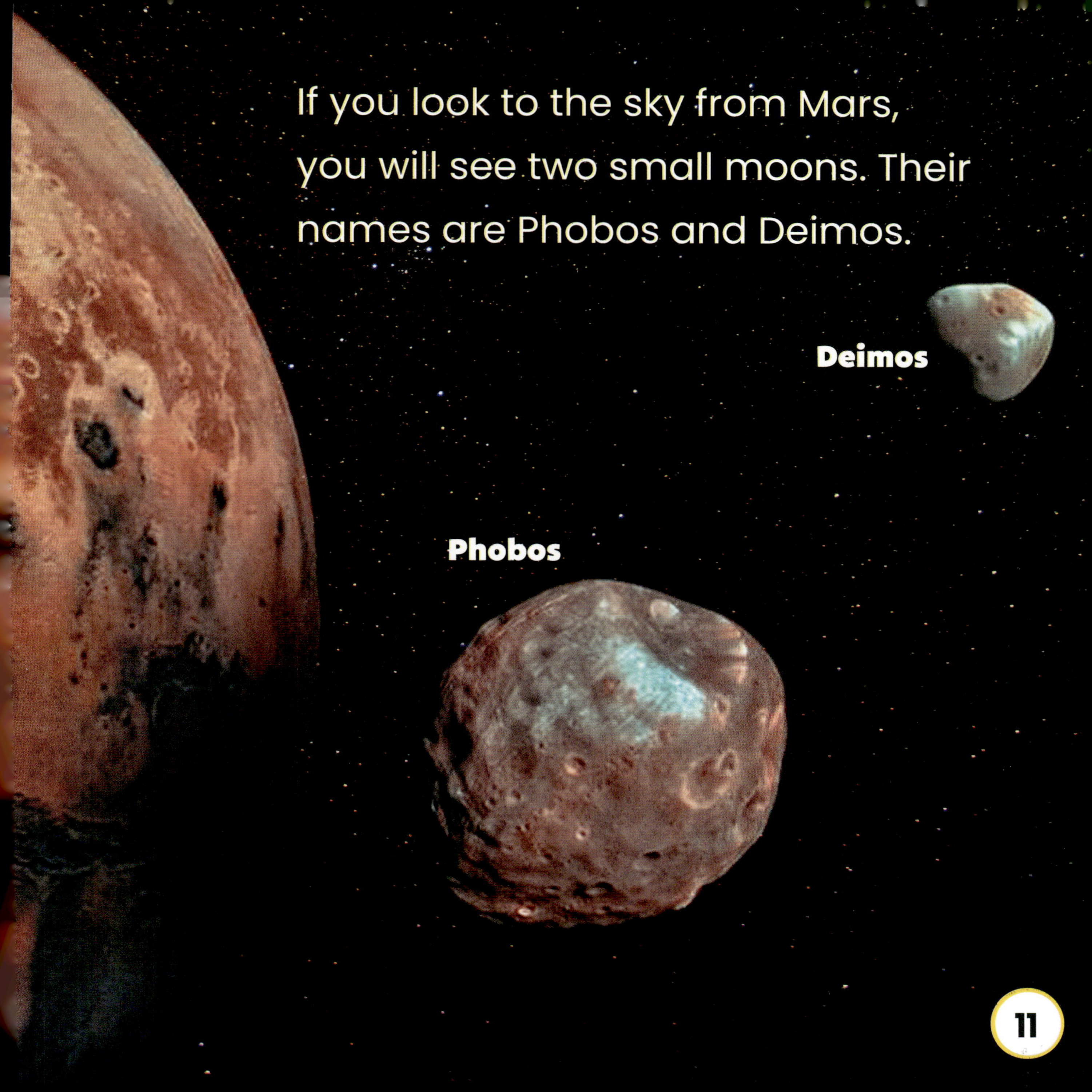

If you look to the sky from Mars, you will see two small moons. Their names are Phobos and Deimos.

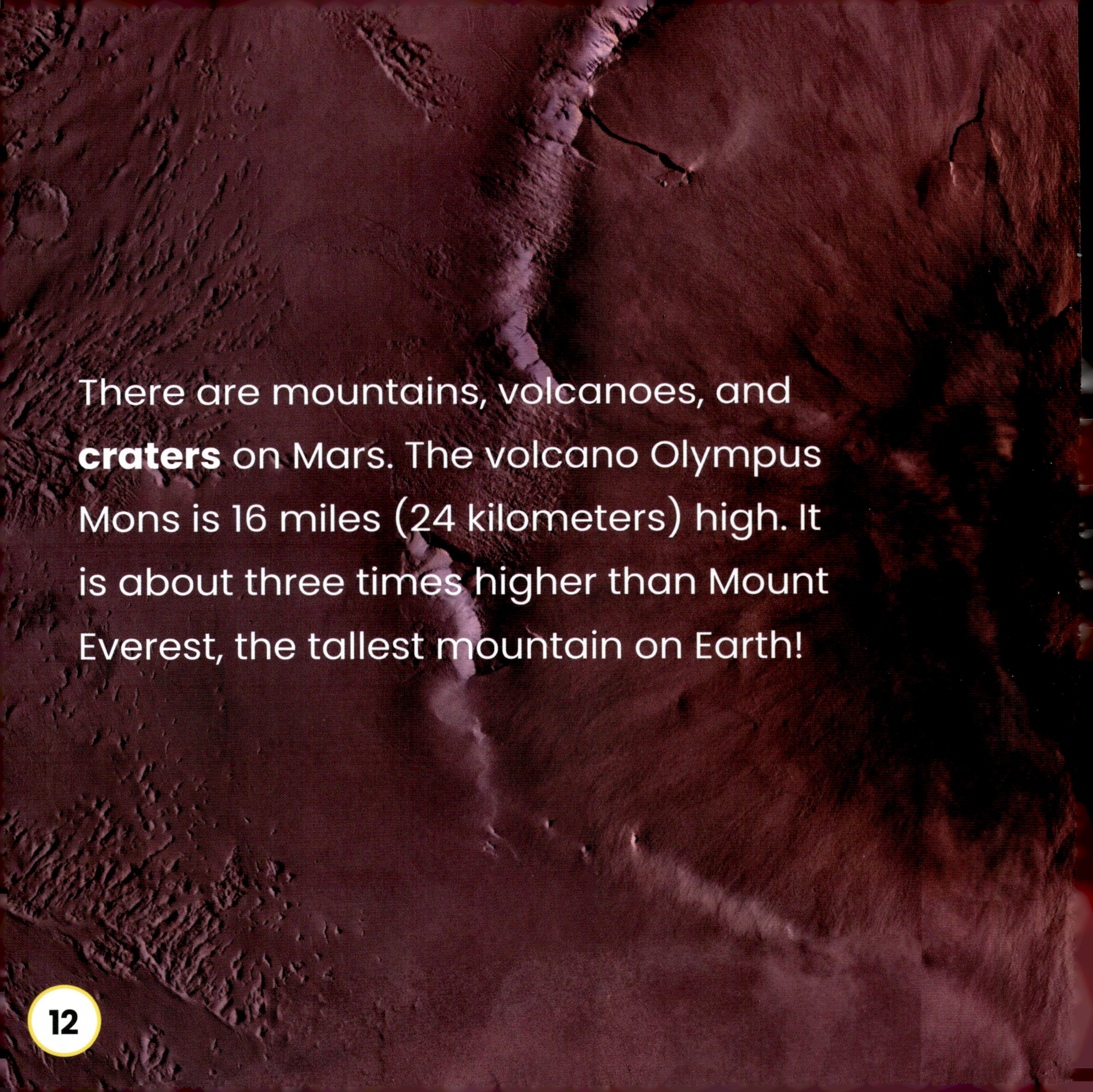

There are mountains, volcanoes, and **craters** on Mars. The volcano Olympus Mons is 16 miles (24 kilometers) high. It is about three times higher than Mount Everest, the tallest mountain on Earth!

Mount Everest
Olympus Mons

Gravity on Mars is weaker than it is on Earth. On Mars, you could jump over five feet (two meters) into the air!

Scientists think Mars formed about five billion years ago. It started as a large spinning disk of dust and gas. Over time, it became a planet.

Some astronomers think Mars was very different long ago. It may have been warmer. There may have been oceans.

Has Mars Been Explored?

Mars is being explored by the robots who live there! Scientists have sent robotic **rovers** to study Mars. The robot Perseverance began exploring the planet in 2021.

The rovers gather rock and soil samples. They send photos and other information back to Earth. **Satellites** also orbit Mars to take pictures and collect data.

Scientists want to know if living things could survive on Mars. They want to figure out how to send human explorers to the red planet.

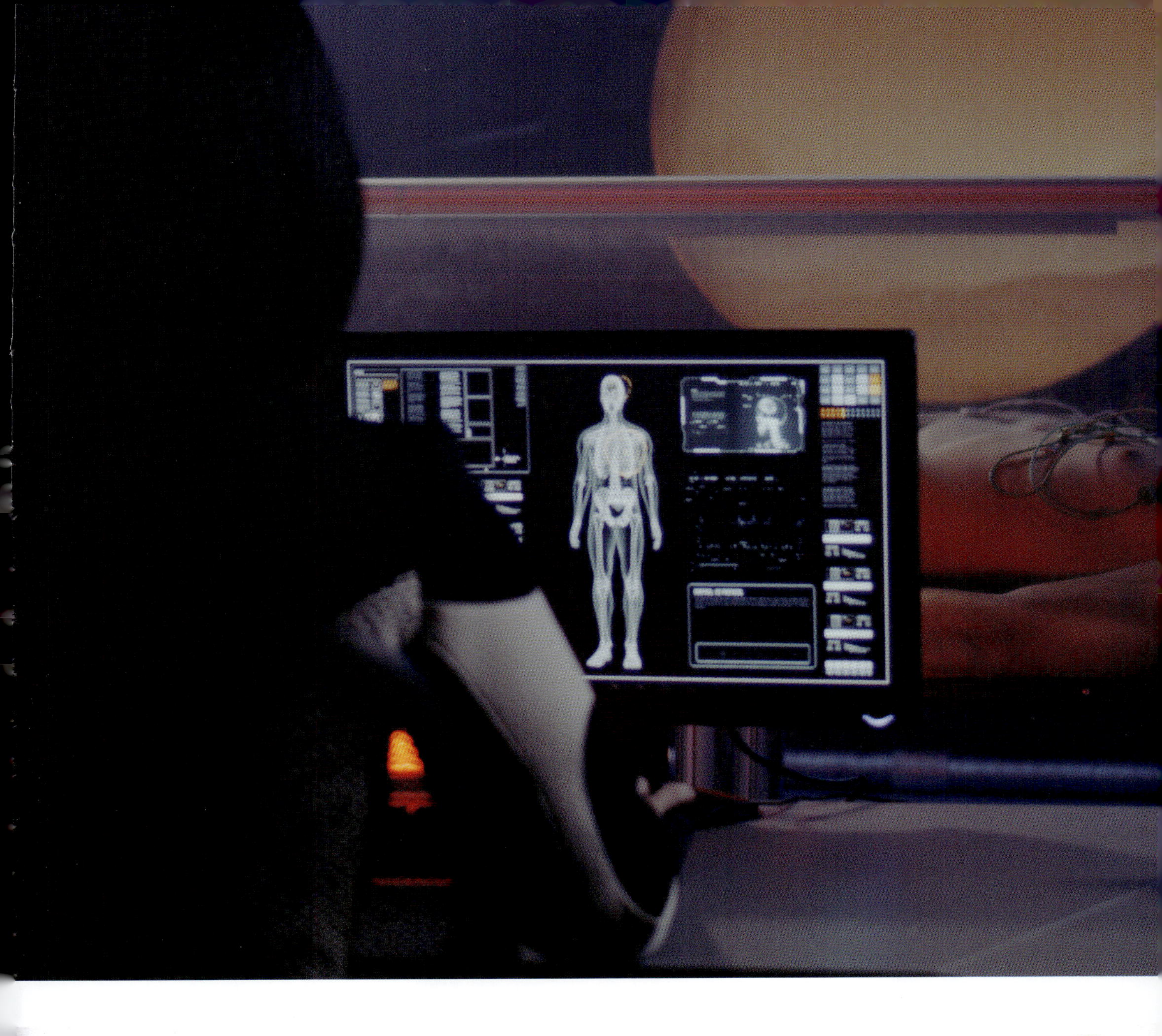

Glossary

astronomer (uh-STRAH-nuh-mer): a scientist who studies objects in the sky, including planets, galaxies, and stars

craters (KRAY-turz): large holes in the ground caused by the impact of something falling or exploding, such as a meteorite crashing or a volcano erupting

gravity (GRAV-i-tee): an invisible force that pulls objects toward each other and keeps them from floating away

orbit (OR-bit): to move in a curved path around a larger body in space

rovers (ROH-vuhrz): robotic vehicles sent to the surfaces of moons and planets to roam and explore

satellites (SAT-uh-lites): spacecrafts sent into orbit around a planet, moon, or other object in space

solar system (SOH-lur SIS-tuhm): the Sun and everything that orbits around it

telescope (TEL-uh-skope): an instrument that helps people see distant objects

terrestrial (tuh-RES-tree-uhl): made up of rocks or minerals and having a hard surface

Thinking Questions

1. Where did the planet Mars get its name?
2. Describe the surface of Mars.
3. How do scientists think Mars formed?
4. In what ways is Mars like Earth?
5. How do rovers help scientists explore Mars?

Index

astronomers 9, 17

Earth 4, 6, 12, 15, 19

Galilei, Galileo 9

gravity 15

moons 11

Olympus Mons 12, 13

orbit 7, 19

rovers 18, 19

Sun 4–7

volcanoes 12

About the Author

Murray "Oak" Tapeta was born in a cabin without plumbing in Montana. Growing up in the great outdoors, he became a lover of nature. He earned the nickname "Oak" after climbing to the top of an oak tree at the age of three. Oak loves to read and write. He has written many books about events in history and other subjects that fascinate him. He prefers spending time in the wilderness with his dog Birchy.